IF WE HIRE FOR STRENGTHS, WHY DO WE MANAGE FOR WEAKNESS?

Al Dawson

If We Hire for Strengths,
Why Do We Manage for Weakness?

First publication: October 2019
Issued in print and electronic formats.
Print: 978-1-9992341-0-2
Electronic: 978-1-9992341-1-9

Dawson, Al, 1973–, author
If We Hire for Strengths / Al Dawson

Editor: Karen Crosby, Editarians

TABLE OF CONTENTS

INTRODUCTION:

THE HIRING FAIRY TALE

Once upon a time, a hiring manager chose to hire a new employee, thrilled that this person would perform well, contribute ideas, and be a model of employee engagement, and everyone on the team lived happily ever after.

Have you heard that story? It's a fairy tale, right?

How about this one: Once upon a time, a hiring manager chose to hire a new employee, thrilled that this person would somehow fall short of performance expectations and need to be set straight with regular pep talks and interventions.

Oh. You haven't heard the story told that way? Me neither. Nobody gets hired for doing what they are not good at.

Sure, we have all been asked questions during an interview along the lines of "What do you suck at?" to see if we have a sense of our own limitations. But as I have in the past, you likely researched some answers online to find out what the interviewer was looking to get from this question, and then you answered accordingly.

Not once in my years of business have I heard of anyone focusing on weaknesses during an interview. More to the point, I have never heard of anyone hiring an employee because this new addition to the team wasn't quite up to snuff. People are always proud of their hires because of what those individuals have done well in the past. It becomes a bit of a boasting game.

A sample hiring notice might look like this:

> *We are very excited to welcome Jane Doe to the team in the role of brand manager. Jane joins us with over 20 years of experience in marketing and 10 years in branding. Jane has played fundamental roles in the branding of such companies as ABC, XYZ, and 123. We are very excited about Jane's knowledge and ability to introduce a different point of view. Jane graduated from the University of Guelph with a master's in marketing in 2005. Since that time, she has worked for some major marketing firms like Erin and Gabe, Page, and, most recently, Frankie and Lola's Branding. Please help me in welcoming Jane to our team. Her first day will be Monday, October 18.*

Yet despite initial enthusiasm, odds are that as managers, we end up managing the weaknesses we didn't hire for.

As Jim Collins pointed out in *Good to Great*, "First who … then what."[1] In other words, first you want to hire great people; after that, you can determine what you want them to do.

So, if we hire people for their strengths, and we're pretty sure we've got the right people, why does the fairy tale happy ending seem so elusive? Why do we end up managing the weaknesses of the people in our care? In this easy-to-read, lighthearted book, I explore this paradox. I provide insight into a paradigm shift, and I give you some tips to help you along your own creative path to managing strengths.

Gallup has identified that only 15% of workers are engaged in

[1] Jim Collins, *Good to Great: Why Some Companies Make the Leap…and Others Don't* (New York: Random House Business, 2001).

their work and get to do at least one thing they enjoy doing each day.[2] It has been proven over and over that if people do what they love, they'll love what they do. Tasks no longer feel like work, which leads to a happier, healthier workplace—and a more profitable, flourishing business.

In these pages, I show you how helping your team stay focused on their strengths can provide them with that opportunity for enjoyment and change the dynamics of your business.

In effect, I help you to write a whole new story. If you've ever read a fairy tale before, I think you're going to love where this is going…

[2] Jim Clifton, "The World's Broken Workplace," *The Chairman's Blog* (blog), *Gallup*, June 12, 2017, https://news.gallup.com/opinion/chairman/212045/world-broken-workplace.aspx

1

IF WE HIRE FOR STRENGTHS, WHY DO WE MANAGE FOR WEAKNESS?

If we hire for strengths, why do we manage for weakness? Well, that's a great question. From my first day in management, I was always told to make sure that employees were doing things right.

For me, that advice didn't mean much other than (a) watching to see if employees were not doing what I thought they were supposed to be doing, and (b) changing their actions by telling them what they were doing wrong and what I wanted them to do instead. That was me, as a supervisor for a national pizza chain. I was thrown into the position, with no real formal training, and some of my friends in comparable positions had even less training.

I was promoted into my management position, and perhaps you were promoted into yours, by knowing what I know and being able to execute tasks. Sometimes, people are promoted simply because they were there—not in my case or yours, I hope—but I see it all the time.

As we mature, we are given more responsibility. This happens not thanks to our skill set, or our aptitude at developing and creating a team, but for what we have *prevented* from happening. Then one day, *whammo*! You are managing a business, a department, or a team. Talk about excitement. Along with the excitement come fear, nervousness, and, usually, sheer chaos, at least for a little while. Eventually you learn how to effectively hire, direct, correct, control, and (unfortunately sometimes) fire people.

What has this promotion process taught us? It has taught us that through this transformation, we are largely left to flounder on our own. In my case, I went from washing dishes to managing a business, but not once did someone talk to me about how to manage people (how to *really* manage people). On more than one occasion I was given tips on how to "manage people," and I attended several courses on this topic, but more often than not I learned about how to correct people's actions, in a manner that hopefully would not offend anyone, and how to set a clear understanding of what is expected.

This approach started off as what was called a shit sandwich. Give your employees a nice piece of bread (by telling them one thing they have done right), then spread on the shit (by telling them what they did wrong), then finish off the conversation with a second piece of bread (by giving them vote of confidence that they can achieve what you have just told them to do). Last, we send the employees off. We hope they have learned what they did wrong and retained our advice on how to make it better moving forward.

Now, what did this sandwich method of management get you? A lot of the time, it got you a successful business that met your customers' expectations. It got you a sense of accomplishment that your business did not fall off the rails, at least for that day, and some of the time, it would get you a business that grew. Depending on the level of fear that you were able to instill in your employees, your business grew substantially.

Wait a minute—did I just say fear? I sure did.

I recognize that as a manager of people, and as a person having been managed by several different people, fear still plays a role today in how we get tasks accomplished and change behaviors in employees.

Behaviors? That is what we are ultimately trying to change. A change in behavior is a sustainable change, as long as it comes from within. (We will get to this later.)

As humans evolve and get a better understanding of what we want, we are learning (at least those who want to) that people are not motivated by fear, unless they are in an unfortunate economic state that forces them to stick to what they have. The bad news about that economic state is that it will end, and if you create a sense of fear in your employees for their actions, they are probably going to end up stealing from you. The theft could come in different ways, given the opportunity, whether it be time, goods, or services.

Along with the theft, you will have employees who will not work in your best interest. Given the chance, they will screw you over by quitting without adequate notice, tainting the work environment by talking ill about their treatment while at work, sabotaging relations with your customers, talking to strangers about their past work environment, and preventing great people from applying at your business. Ultimately, they can hurt your brand and business as an employer and commerce partner.

So, what should we do? Well, what do you think would be different if we managed strengths? By focusing on what your team members are doing well, you not only encourage positive behaviors, but you create a culture where thoughtful risk is encouraged and success is the norm.[3] What does this mean? This means that by focusing solely on what your employees are doing well, they not only continue to outperform the average person in their area, but their self-confidence will be greatly enhanced. They begin to tackle different areas of your business, and their life, with a better attitude and strengthened certainty toward their ability to complete the tasks ahead of them.

Sounds pretty simple, right? Well, it is.

With this change in mindset, your employees will quickly become

---

[3] Caveat: I encourage people never to talk down to others, even in the most dangerous of situations, but I believe firmly that sometimes people need to be told what to do for their own health and safety or that of your customers. These areas of your business should be clearly identified and non-negotiable.

team members, and their level of contribution increase tenfold over where it is currently. Talk about return on investment. For a $0.00 investment, absolutely nothing financial, your business will start to see better productivity and cost control, and the overall performance of your employees or your newly created team will improve.

By implementing this change in managing people, you will create a happier work environment, people from all over will want to be a part of your company, and you will have the opportunity to create your so-called dream team of talented people who want to help you achieve your goals for your business. By giving your team the opportunity to have you believe in them, you will have a team whose greatest challenge will be—wait for it—that they need help facilitating their thoughts around their performance, ultimately creating their own path for improvement. Wow! No one is stopping you now.

So, how *do* we manage for strengths? No one said it was going to be easy. Nothing that turns out great results is ever easy. Did you get to the position you are in now because of luck? No, hard work and dedication got you to your current situation, and probably some sacrifice, too. This change in managing people takes a lot of effort because it is easier to point out what is wrong. We do it naturally.

Only the ones who are truly committed to managing for strengths will reap the full rewards. If you choose to do only bits and pieces, things will become better at that rate: what you put in, you will get out. But hey, better is better, and one step in the right direction at least has you moving in the right direction.

A place for my thoughts . . .

2

THE POWER OF HAO

The Power of HAO? Are you wondering what I am talking about? Well, HAO (rhymes with *how*) stands for How to Approach Opportunities. I am talking about the power of a moment in time when you are about to learn something.

I learned the seeds of this philosophy from Benjamin Zander, a conductor for the Boston philharmonic orchestra and one of the authors of the book *Art of Possibilities*.[4]

What I took away from the Zanders' book was only the beginning to what would become a series of questions that led to the Power of HAO, my theory on how to approach opportunities. I learned that if you approach a problem as the beginning to a remarkable lesson, you will welcome it with open arms, ultimately creating a culture where people are not afraid, are encouraged to make mistakes, and are receptive to continuous learning.

This is one piece of managing strengths: make people feel included and comfortable to fail. This theory can be initiated in any way you feel is most suitable for your environment. Depending on your audience, you should make it suit them. I recommend making your approach

[4] Rosamund Zander and Benjamin Zander, *Art of Possibilities* (Boston: Harvard Business School Press, 2000).

as silly as you are comfortable with—ensuring a continued level of professionalism—so that it absolutely removes all apprehension about any "mistakes" being made and any problems that might arise.

For example, in several circumstances, I have had the opportunity to practice the Power of HAO in the role of a business auditor. At the beginning of the day, I set the expectation for how the day will flow, including the power of surprise. I do so in true Zander style. I tell the team that whenever we see what has to be considered a problem, we will throw our hands up in the air and yell, "How fascinating!"

Setting this expectation accomplishes two things. First, it creates a sense of curiosity. Second, it injects humor into the setting. I then explain the rules for the "how fascinating" moments, emphasizing that by using this approach for the audit, we should definitely raise some eyebrows and encourage an environment of fun.

Moving into the day, during our collaborative audit we invariably come across our first so-called problem. With our arms waving, we yell, "How fascinating!" The team's first reaction is usually shock, followed by curiosity and amusement. After a couple more bursts, the team starts to accept and even invite this behavior.

The overall environment during the business audit using the Power of HAO—which is typically extremely stressful—becomes one of fun and acceptance. People are given the comfort and space to do what they naturally do best, as opposed to what they think they should be doing.

This is one example of how this approach can been used in a stressful setting for multiple people. The managers who have continued to use the Power of HAO have seen a significant improvement in the day-to-day operations of their business through team morale, engagement, willingness to participate—and results.

Of note, in these companies, team members' willingness to be open about what is happening or has happened has changed significantly for the better, providing more conversation and an openness that allows momentum to carry forward quickly. In the past, team members would try to hide what they were doing if they felt (or knew) it was wrong, or thought they might be blamed or criticized. Under the new approach, problems or mistakes are celebrated (and then solved). Instituting the Power of HAO has the ability to create a culture shift to one where mistakes are celebrated and the team's confidence is strengthened.

The key to the success of this program is the follow-up that takes place right after this magical moment of finding a problem. (More on this topic later.)

Of course, when I've used this approach for the first time in an organization, I'm prepared for the team to have some questions about it. My general response is that I'm trying something new. "I think we can pull it off," I tell them.

A common question is a concern about setting a poor precedent: if people aren't taking mistakes seriously, won't that lead to more of them? No. Paradoxically, it eventually leads to fewer.

Have you heard the story of Rule #6? Two prime ministers (PMs) are sitting in an office talking when one of the hosting PM's aides comes running into the room.

"Sir! Sir!" exclaims the aide.

He is interrupted by the hosting PM. "John, please remember Rule #6."

"Ah, yes sir," says the aide, and calmly walks away.

A few minutes pass and the same thing happens with a different aide. "Sir, sir! I—"

Again, she is interrupted by the hosting PM. "Mary, please remember Rule #6."

"Yes, sir," she says, immediately returning to a state of calm and leaving the room.

A few minutes pass as the PMs continue to talk. Finally, the visiting PM cannot contain his curiosity any longer. "What I've just seen is remarkable. What is Rule 6?"

"Ah, it's quite easy," the hosting PM replies. "Don't take yourself so seriously."

"What are the other rules?" asks the visiting PM.

"There aren't any."

Underlying the Power of HAO is the foundational belief that you should not take yourself seriously, yet you should take what you do very seriously. If your team really starts homing in on their strengths and *using* them, they will feel challenged, fulfilled, and appreciated.

It is amazing to watch how behaviors change as your team gains confidence and understands that you will not be instigating any repercussions for them having made mistakes out of curiosity. They wander (and wonder) into other areas of your business and take an interest in what other team members are doing, giving them at a minimum an understanding of how others in your organization impact the overall customer experience. These changes in mindset make team members more efficient in their roles and give them the self-assurance to help in other areas when needed.

Another question I often hear about this approach pertains to image: what will our customers think when they hear that team members are having fun with mistakes at their expense? Initially, customers are shocked when someone doesn't appear to be taking what just happened to them seriously. As soon as the customers start to realize what is happening, however, their demeanor changes. In some cases, they start to get involved in the process. They start cheering. Imagine a world where your customers are engaged in their own solutions!

In other circumstances, customers simply accept the actions of the team as this approach slowly becomes the culture of the business. Either way, customers notice an improvement in the overall vibe—and service levels—of the business. Right away, as soon as the perceived problem is resolved, customers, in their own spirit of learning, often start asking team members about their perplexing behaviors.

In follow-up conversations and visits to businesses that have adopted the Power of HAO, the message is consistent:

The leaders are saying,

> *"It has changed not only how I react to situations at work, but it has made me an all-around more positive person. My family has noticed a difference in my personal life."*

The team members are saying,

> *"Work is a lot more relaxed these days. I feel more comfortable about what I am doing. I feel that management is working with me, not against me."*

What a great thought. Your team is actually enjoying work by doing what they are good at and being recognized for it. They are learning and managing their own performance and striving to be better at what they do. Your team will enjoy doing more of what gets them the recognition they desire, implementing more of what works, and playing to their strengths.

Your response can improve their self-confidence, leading to an environment in which they take calculated risks based on their strengths and self-correct based on what is already working. This positive spiral presents a whole new situation within the business: an improved bottom line.

How can you approach opportunities?_What actions can you take right now to help you down this path? . . .

3

WHAT DO YOU WANT?

Asking what you want sounds like a pretty easy question. Ironically, trying to figure it out takes a lot of hard work, time, and commitment. Most businesspeople have not taken the time to complete this step for a variety of reasons: they have never been challenged to do so, they don't see the importance, or they're short on time due to a lack of planning, and it shows in their business over and over again. If you do not start with clarity on what you want, you will never get there.

Before we dive into the details, though, it's important for you and your team to recognize and celebrate what is already working. Not everything you are currently doing needs to change. No way! A lot of what you are doing is likely to be working quite well, or else you would not be where you are.

Make sure you and your team take some time to focus on the strengths you already have. By reflecting on what's working well before you get focused on what you want to change, you will likely be inspired by what is already successful, and you will have an existing framework of processes and steps to refer to when it comes time to implement what you are about to discover over the next two chapters. You will also quickly be reminded how awesome you really are.

Figuring out what you want starts with visualization. With your team, get as detailed as you can: visualize what people are wearing, what they are saying and doing, what you are saying and doing, how you are reacting to situations that arise in this preferred outcome, how people are going to know you have reached this desired outcome, and how you're going to celebrate. Be clear in determining your priorities, as this is an important step if you are to achieve substantial results.

Once you think you have figured out what you want, dig deeper and start to picture what will be happening around you when you have achieved your goal or desired outcome.

This visualization exercise is a crucial step in the successful growth of your business. If you and your team are not crystal clear on your goals (desired outcome), then you will be unable to achieve them strategically. Once you have the vision of the desired outcome, you can start working backwards to now.

Let's say you want highly satisfied customers. As part of the visualization exercise, you determine what your future customers are saying about your business. This vision should align with your core values as an individual and as a company. Once you have that clear vision, the team can start to figure out what needs to happen to achieve it.

If one component of your vision is that your customers will refer to your company as timely, you then collaborate to figure out what your customers expect in terms of timeliness. For example, is it to reply to any customer-initiated correspondence within twenty-four hours? Five hours? Which one of these is your customer going to consider timely?

Next, working backwards, the team can then start to discuss how this expectation could be achieved. When you are in this mode, think in terms of possibilities. How could this goal be reached? Now you have set the internal expectation and can train against it.

At this point of the process, your words become your badge. In other words, what you say will become the reality for your organization. As Henry Ford said, "Whether you think you can or think you can't, you're right."

If you choose your words carefully around the preferred future, you will have an easier time in achieving the desired outcome. If you focus on what could go wrong, things will end up going wrong. Your words should be chosen based on positive results, not hurdles. Remember, you are managing strengths, starting from a position of what is already working.

Having this focus is not to say that we should not acknowledge hurdles. We need to acknowledge hurdles, as they are a part of reality, but we should speak about the hurdles once they have arisen as if you have overcome them. To speak about the hurdle in a positive way brings you back to the beginning of this chapter. What do you want?

For example, if the goal is to cross the road and the hurdle is traffic, your goal-oriented statement could be, "When the traffic breaks, we will cross the road." Notice that the first word sets the tone. The word *when* leads you to believe that the crossing is going to take place. *When* creates certainty. If we swap a word not focused on the desired outcome, such as *if*, the overall feeling of the statement changes. "If the traffic breaks, we will cross the road" becomes a possibility statement. It leaves you with a sense of hope, not certainty.

From there, keep moving backwards in the process of what you and your team are going to do to achieve the collaborative goals. For example, let's say your timeliness goal is to have all correspondence returned within five hours. Well, for the team to achieve this goal, what are they going to need? If we are talking about email, would a mobile device give them the ability to make this goal realistic? What about the use of an auto responder? What else would be needed? Lastly, is the team committed to the vision? Chapter 5 talks about how…

I end this chapter with this question for you to ponder: how will people know you have reached your goal? (Hint: You have to know what you want first.)

What do you want? . . .

4

WHAT DO YOU REALLY WANT?

You might be thinking, "What do I want? I thought you just asked me that." Well, sort of. But now the question is, "What do you *really* want?"

Visualization provides an understanding of what you want on the surface. You have painted a picture in theory. It's time to get out the brushes to create it in reality. So, the next part is figuring out the details: what needs to happen so that the goal outlined is sustainable? That's it! This chapter is about the actual behaviors that need to change to make your goals achievable and sustainable and why these behaviors are important.

What is a behavior, anyway? Behavior, defined by Merriam-Webster, is the way in which someone conducts oneself or behaves; the manner of conducting oneself; the response of an individual, group, or species to its environment.[5]

At this stage you should have the desired outcome detailed, the steps outlined to achieve the outcome, and, most importantly, buy-in

[5] *Merriam-Webster Online*, s.v. "behavior," accessed October 20, 2019, https://www.merriam-webster.com/dictionary/behavior.

from all involved. The next questions revolve around the behaviors that need to change.

Start by looking at your current state and celebrating your successes in getting this far. Celebrating success is an important way to bring out more of what is working and catapult a team's or individual's strengths. From this point, pose the following style of question:

"Where do we want to be tomorrow, or in thirty, sixty, and ninety days?"

"How will we notice we have achieved our goal?"

These questions deepen your thought process about your goal, and all are focused on the outcome. I hope, by now, you are realizing that you will achieve your goal(s).

What beliefs do you have around your current state, your desired outcome, and each step along the way? How will they be different when you have achieved the first step? What difference will your and your team's selected behaviors have on other areas of your business, or your personal lives? How will people notice that you have moved forward? What behaviors are going to change to get you and your team there?

For an example of how this works, let's go back to the timely response goal. What are the behaviors that as a team we need to change? Is the behavior we are exhibiting one of avoidance? Is that why people are not getting back to customers in a timely manner? What behavior do we want instead? Confrontation? Discipline? What about pursuit? Which one represents us best? Now you are cooking with gas! You are so on the way to sustainable change…

Once you have decided what is right for you, the next series of questions could look like this:

If pursuit is our desired behavior, how would we recognize that behavior in someone?

What would that person do differently?

What am I willing to do differently?

What small change can we make as a team, or can I make as a person, that will get us (or me) heading in that direction?

So why is this chapter about behaviors? Because behaviors automatically drive us to do what we do. If you display avoidance behaviors in one area of your life, chances are you will display some form of that behavior in everything you do. Identifying what behaviors you want instead, and working toward changing them, will help you achieve not only your desired outcome but improvements in all aspects of your life that the desired behavior can support.

What do you really want?. . .

5

WHO MADE YOU THE EXPERT?

Who made you the expert? What a weird question. But it's a good one. As in so many things, we think that because we have the title, we ought to know what we are doing. If we're not sure, we do what others have done. As managers of people, then, we tell them what to do. As a result, we find ourselves having the same conversations and dealing with the same things over and over again instead of moving forward. This management style, although effective for immediate results, does not get you sustainable change with a purpose.

The alternative is to use a collaborative approach to generate solutions and manage people. A collaborative solution is such a powerful alternative, it deserves its own name: a *collaborution*. You will get a wide variety of different points of view, perhaps even some off-the-wall ideas that you or any other brainiac would never have thought of. Chances are that if you involve your team in finding a solution, you will get not only a great solution, but one that will last because the team that has to work with it created it. A great solution with staying power is the hallmark of a well-executed collaborution.

This process is simple . . . but it's not easy. Actually, it can be a difficult discipline if you are not used to it. When a problem has presented itself to you and your team, after you have thrown your arms up in delight, let the questions begin and engage your genuine curiosity and respect for your team as the work begins.

The first question that should be posed to the entire team is, "What outcomes do we want instead of this one?" Once the desired outcome has been determined, you can start moving forward, as explained in previous chapters.

The first few times you ask this question, you might find yourself quite stressed out. Actually, if you are not used to it, it is a hard question to answer. The process should not lead you to a simple solution, but rather give you the opportunity to figure out the perfect desired outcome for this situation. A collaborution.

If it is a simple problem with a simple solution, then great, but chances are that the issues needing attention in your workplace will evolve into long-term goals. Sure, there will be short-term milestones that need to be achieved along the way to the ultimate scenario, but the vision will be set. Creating the desired outcome together helps to carve the goal in stone, and because it was created collaboratively, the likelihood of it being achieved will be significantly greater. It has been proven that if the team feels part of the solution, then the chances of them buying in and working toward the desired outcome will be greatly enhanced.

While working through this process with your team, remember that your idea might not be the right one. The goal is to come up with the best idea for your business, and one that your entire team supports. This means that sometimes, your idea might be left behind. It does not mean you are any less of a manager or leader. On the contrary, it means that you are a stronger leader and that you have surrounded yourself with smart people. Both are important to the long-term sustainability of your business. Great things in business are never done by one person; they are done by teams of people. That includes solutions.

As we learned in previous chapters, after you have created the desired outcome, the next step in this process is to plan backwards from that vision. What steps are needed to achieve the preferred future? Your plan is complete when the first small step that will lead you down the path is clear and you are willing to take it.

Small steps are important for two reasons. First, when we take and celebrate successful small steps, we continue to build self-esteem and create a sense of accomplishment. If the goal is long-term, we then have lots of reasons to celebrate. Second, creating and taking small steps allows us to reconvene as a group and change directions quickly if something isn't working. Thus, small steps in the right direction over a long period of time create a big difference,[6] whereas a small step in the wrong direction changed right away does not have a significant impact on the long-term goal.

I wonder what would be different in your organization if as a team you were constantly celebrating successes? What difference would that orientation have on team morale and turnover? How could this approach change your business trajectory?

Let's talk about the impact great morale and lowered turnover would have on customer satisfaction. If you take care of your team, your team will take care of your customer, and your customer will take care of you. The best part about the collaborative approach to solutions process is that as you manage performance, you increase morale, and a virtuous cycle begins on two levels. The first is outlined above: celebrating small wins builds capacity. The second is that ensuring your team has well-defined goals gives them something to strive for. People inherently want to achieve goals, especially ones that they have helped to create. If you let your team co-create goals and know the impact of them, they will rise to be a part of the overall solutions.

---

[6] As Gary Keller and Jay Papasan wrote in *The ONE Thing* (Austin: Rellek Publishing Partners, 2012), a two-inch domino can knock over a domino 50% larger, such that the tenth domino would be as tall as a grown man, the eighteenth would match the Leaning Tower of Pisa, the thirty-first would loom over Mount Everest, and the fifty-seventh would almost reach the moon.

What positive changes can you see by including more people in solutions? By embracing collaborution?

6

SO, WHAT ARE YOU GOING TO DO DIFFERENTLY?

This is where what you have learned and retained so far becomes truly your game. What is your commitment to make things better? As mentioned in Chapter 1, your team's results will be related to the effort, both mental and physical, put into achieving them. Your team is going to be a part of what you want them to be a part of.

You need to do what is right for you and your business. Think about the desired outcome before you start moving or give direction. Challenge yourself to solicit feedback from your team and your customers, and get them involved in the solutions that will affect the long-term growth of your business.

My best hope for you is that as the leader of a business, you will create an environment in which you and your team construct collaborutions based on the long-term preferred future for your business. Your people will be a part of a group that strengthens them daily.

Back to what is right for you. What you do differently is going to define the future path for your business. As the saying goes, "Insanity is doing the same thing over and over again, and expecting different results." How are you going to notice that things are different? How will your team notice that things are different? What is your first small step to creating these proven changes?

Continue to celebrate every step. If we stay still, we languish. Whether it is a right or wrong step, at least it is a step. You can always correct course. Take your time to craft an individualized solution—custom-made by you, for you.

What is your first small step?...

7

CELEBRATION

Celebrations are a big and important part of the equation. This is especially so during the discovery phase, yet not limited to it. As you or members of your team try different things, make sure that you celebrate all along the way.

This part of the process is critical. You are celebrating brave moments, fearful moments, breakthroughs, and failures that will turn into learning moments. You are celebrating movement and building up people's strengths. Remember that some of the world's most notable items—such as Corn Flakes, Post-it Notes, Teflon, and penicillin—were all discovered by mistake. Imagine if those people or teams had not taken a moment to celebrate and ask more questions about what had just happened?

All the work leading up to celebratory moments can be tough and tiring. That said, you need to make this ongoing part of the process obvious: every chance you get, let team members know that what they are doing is working. If it is not working, the course can be easily corrected. What they are doing matters, and it matters that you and your customers recognize their work.

Here, be specific about your language. Words matter. They need to be genuine and complimentary. Your words need to focus on what is working as this is critical to them having meaning. For example, you might say:

> *"Jane, I am really impressed by how you stepped outside your comfort zone to try to close that deal. I specifically liked how you started the conversation by getting to know the client and understanding his needs. Congratulations."*

> *"Taylor, I am very happy to see you go out of your way to make that guest feel special. By listening to the guest fully before you responded, you ensured that she felt heard and understood. That is the kind of behavior we need more of."*

Celebration does not mean monetary reward. On the contrary, it means that you celebrate success by recognizing contributions and the forward momentum at every moment possible during your journey.

Continued celebrations, culminating in the final celebration, forge a culture that everyone wants to be a part of. People will work hard to keep moving forward. If celebration is not taken seriously and completed in its entirety, you will waste effort and end up at the point of your last celebration. If your industry moves quickly due to market trends, supplier availability, or the like, targets may shift frequently. In that environment, celebrating along the way keeps engagement high even if the original outcome is never met. After all, you will still be closer to where you want to be.

It is critical to recognize that this process is iterative: the end is the beginning. The final celebration is the indicator that you have achieved your preferred outcome, which becomes the starting point of what you are already doing well when you undertake your next change initiative. The final celebration really marks the beginning of the next preferred future to be crafted.

What are some things you could celebrate that you haven't yet?...

CLOSURE

What should I say? I feel as though we have been through so much together. I truly wish you continued success—to whatever level you want to reach. I hope that in this quick read, you have found some ideas that will help you in your travels of owning a business or managing people.

Remember that people inherently want to do a good job and be recognized for their contributions. Your task is to set them up for success by giving them the opportunity to harness their strengths to benefit your business. Following the formula outlined in this book will ultimately give you and your team more confidence, more capacity, and more courage to take calculated risks to add value to your customers and your business.

Food for thought: Your relationship with your customers is only as good as the relationship between you and your team. If you want your goals to come alive, then you must live the vision as if you have already achieved it. If you live your words, they will become your reality and your successes.

That's it.

It is that simple in theory. The hard part is in the execution, and the execution is in the commitment. To whatever level you take this process, strive to create an environment in which you are managing, engaging, and celebrating strengths. Ensure that people are doing what they are strong at. Having that focus is going to make your journey, and theirs, so much easier and more enjoyable.

And they all lived happily ever after.

ACKNOWLEDGMENTS

I would like to thank a few people for their help and leadership in my life and in the lessons I've learned along the way.

First and most importantly, Fiona, you have been such a supporter of me, even when I was not. Your commitment to us has allowed me to take chances in chasing my "today" dreams. This has been such a blessing, and I am forever grateful. I love you. Taylor and Delaney, thank you for bringing me joy. When I have been stressed, you have somehow found the right time to show up, make sure I breathe normally, and play for just long enough.

Haesun Moon, you opened my eyes to such a wonderful way of thinking, talking, and leading people. Using a solutions-focused approach in my day-to-day interactions with colleagues, friends, and family has allowed me to remain steadfast yet move with more agility and certainty to get closer to a desired future.

To Karen Crosby, you have been such a wonderful editor and coach throughout this process. I am thankful for your skill set in helping me fine tune my writing and making me proud of this project.

Finally, to the people I have worked with, thank you for having the confidence in me to let me lead, and the trust to be led. You have all been my guinea pigs at some point. You all knew that, though.

ABOUT THE AUTHOR

What can we say about Al Dawson? Professionally, Al is an accomplished and empathetic executive with over 25 years of success in leading business operations, organizational change, and team and strategy development. His consulting experience ranges from complex, multi-stakeholder environments in such renowned corporations as Tim Hortons (Restaurant Brands International), Fairmont Hotels & Resorts, Pizza Hut, and Panago Pizza to entrepreneurial small and medium-sized businesses. Al's business legacy has been results driven and solution focused, with a strong history of partnership development, people leadership, and business growth in a style all his own.

It is easy to talk about what makes an individual great when one lists professional credentials and experience built over years of lessons learned and challenges overcome, but what differentiates Al is who he is at heart. It sounds cheesy, perhaps, in the bio of a professional business book, but his caring is his keystone characteristic: without it, none of the credentials and experience build up to anything lasting. Al's success lies in his ability to show his team, stakeholders, business partners, and colleagues that he truly cares—about getting the job done right and achieving results, of course, but most importantly about not sacrificing the importance of people in the process. Those important relationships create the environment of corporate success day in and day out. Al always has your back and your bottom line!

Al has a knack for injecting pleasure into the business equation. He has fun, and it is important to him that the people he works with and for have fun, too. He is a true optimist in business and in life. As Disney's CEO Bob Iger says, nobody wants to work for a pessimist.

Al currently lives in Manitoba, Canada, with his lovely wife, Fiona; his two daughters, Taylor and Delaney; and Oliver, the family dog. Al is the world's greatest dad (or so he's been told) and a perfectly imperfect husband (the best kind). The family's personal and professional ventures have taken them to various places throughout Canada and have given them the pleasure of working with and meeting many exceptional people.

For more information and resources on managing for strengths, visit https://www.ifwehireforstrengths.com

To reach Al, Please go to www.ifwehireforstrengths.com for all communication and links to social media platforms.

Manufactured by Amazon.ca
Bolton, ON

39452938R00024